Managing Disruptions in AWS Serverless Application Repository

Table of Contents

Chapter 1. Introduction

These days, management of disruptions in the AWS Serverless Application Repository is deemed to be a crucial aspect of businesses' online operations, as it ensures a smooth, seamless digital experience for both employees and customers. Our special report delves into this high-stake topic with precision, offering comprehensive, easy-to-understand guidelines on mitigating disturbances effectively, ensuring you can stay calm during digital storms, and remain afloat. Drawing upon real world case studies and expert insights, this report demystifies the complexities of managing AWS serverless applications and arms you with the knowledge you need to respond to disruptions swiftly. Even if you don't possess a technical background, this report is designed to translate complex topics into digestible blocks, catering to all levels of understanding. Don't let technical fears hold you back. It's time to step into the future with confidence and a strong handle on AWS serverless applications!

Chapter 2. Understanding AWS Serverless Application Repository: An Introduction

AWS Serverless Application Repository is a managed service that allows developers to deploy, share, and reuse serverless applications. The concept of serverless computing helps to relieve developers from the heavy lifting of managing servers and allows them to focus on their core business logic.

AWS serverless applications are made up of one or more lambda functions—portions of code that are triggered by events, run only when needed, and scale automatically. They deliver computing power without requiring traditional server infrastructure. Being on the serverless platform means that you do not have to worry about provisioning or managing servers.

2.1. The Promise of AWS Serverless Applications

Serverless applications yield some extrusive benefits that make them a lucrative choice.

First, it can be incredibly cost-effective. Thanks to the scalability of AWS Lambda, you only pay for the compute time you consume. No idle time is charged, meaning that if your application receives massive traffic suddenly, AWS will handle the spike and charge only for that period.

Second, serverless applications deliver a significant boost to productivity. They help to streamline workflow, as there is no need to maintain operating systems or manage underlying servers. AWS takes care of all these management operations.

Third, serverless applications foster innovation by allowing developers to focus on building new functionalities rather than worrying about the underlying infrastructure.

Finally, AWS Serverless is secure by default, handling all necessary patching and security management at the infrastructure level.

2.2. Components of AWS Serverless Application

Serverless Applications in AWS consist of four key components: AWS Lambda, Amazon API Gateway, AWS Step Functions, and Amazon DynamoDB.

- AWS Lambda: Lambda is a zero-administration compute platform for back-end web developers that runs your code for you in the AWS cloud and provides you with a fine-grained pricing structure.

- Amazon API Gateway: A fully managed service for creating, publishing, maintaining, and securing APIs at any scale. It helps in handling traffic management, authorization, and access control, and supports monitoring and logging.

- AWS Step Functions: It is a serverless workflow service that lets you orchestrate AWS services and build applications from discrete tasks.

- Amazon DynamoDB: A highly reliable, scalable, and fully managed NoSQL database service.

Each of these components plays a crucial role in the efficient functioning of AWS serverless application architecture.

2.3. Getting Started with AWS Serverless Application Repository

The entry-point to the Serverless Repository is the AWS Management Console. Here, you can search for and deploy pre-existing applications directly to your AWS environment. The key steps involved in getting started are:

1. Starting from the AWS Management Console, navigate to the Serverless Application Repository.

2. Here, you can browse through a wide selection of serverless applications. You can also use the search bar to find an application that matches your requirement.

3. Once you find an application, you can click on it to see a detailed description, including the resources the application will create, permissions it requires, and source code involved.

4. If you are satisfied with the details, you can deploy the application.

2.4. Overview of AWS SAM

AWS SAM (Serverless Application Model) is an open-source framework you can use to build serverless applications on AWS. It provides you with a template specification to define your serverless application and a command-line interface (CLI) tool.

So, how does it play well with the AWS Serverless Application Repository?

AWS SAM is a critical tool to use when creating or modifying serverless applications in the Repository. When you use the AWS SAM CLI to package your application, it builds and packages your code and any dependencies into deployment-ready artifacts. These artifacts are uploaded to an S3 bucket, and a SAM template is returned which references these artifacts. The SAM template can then be used to share your application or library.

2.5. Conclusion

In essence, the AWS Serverless Application Repository, underpinned by AWS Lambda and other AWS tools, offers businesses a flexible and cost-effective platform to build, deploy, and manage their serverless applications. Grasping these concepts will provide a solid foundation for further exploring more advanced topics and use-cases. Understanding serverless applications will not only help businesses stay ahead in the digital race but also enable them to manage disruptions more effectively and efficiently.

Chapter 3. Demystifying Disruptions: Breaking Down the Basics

In this digital era, serverless architectures such as AWS Serverless Application Repository have become the heart and soul of countless online operations. Understanding and managing the potential disruptions in these systems is crucial to ensuring uninterrupted digital experiences. To start, we need to break down the basics.

3.1. Understanding Serverless Applications

Serverless applications are those that heavily depend on third-party services (referred to as Backend as a Service or BaaS) or on custom code that's run in ephemeral containers (Function as a Service or FaaS). AWS Serverless Application Repository is a managed service that makes it easier for developers to discover, configure, and deploy serverless applications and components on AWS. The serverless applications in this repository are packaged configurations of AWS resources, including AWS Lambda functions, and their associated AWS resources.

3.2. Defining Disruptions

Disruptions can be considered as any event that interrupts normal workflow or business operations. In the context of AWS serverless applications, disruptions could mean anything from simple code bugs, infrastructure failures, to unexpected spikes in user demand outpacing resource scaling capabilities.

3.3. The Anatomy of a Serverless Disruption

Imagine the sequence of events when a request is made to a serverless application. The request triggers a function (for instance, an AWS Lambda function), which then interacts with other AWS resources or third-party services, processes the request, and returns a response.

A disruption could occur at various stages in this process. If the function isn't deployed properly or if there is an error in the code, the function might not trigger, leading to a disruption. Similarly, if the downstream resources or services that the function interacts with have issues, it could lead to disruptions.

3.4. Inspecting the Causes of Disruptions

Understanding the root causes of disruptions is key to managing them effectively. Some common causes include:

1. AWS Lambda service disruption: This could be AWS-specific issues causing widespread disruptions to AWS services.

2. Faulty deployments: Mistakes while deploying the application could cause issues.

3. Code bugs: Errors in application code can lead to malfunctions and disruptions.

4. Underscaled resources: If applications are not properly scaled to handle the load, it could result in disruptions.

5. Network issues: Problems with network connectivity or external services may affect application availability and performance.

3.5. Mitigating Serverless Disruptions

When it comes to mitigating disruptions, a multi-pronged approach should be adopted. Having a monitoring and alerting system in place helps in early detection of issues and fixing them before they escalate. Regularly reviewing and updating the application code to prevent bugs is also vital.

In addition, undertaking load testing and performance monitoring to ensure that the applications are well-optimized and can handle spikes in user demand can go a long way in preventing disruptions due to under-scaled resources. Make sure to design application architectures to be resilient, utilizing AWS best practices and services that provide failover and redundancy capabilities.

3.6. A Case Study: AWS Lambda Disruption

Let's consider a real-world case where an AWS Lambda disruption occurred.

One of the largest clothing retailer's e-commerce site experienced a significant downtime during its annual sale. On investigation, it was discovered that the issue originated from an AWS Lambda service disruption. The sudden surge of users overwhelmed the system, and the Lambda functions that handled user requests were unable to scale up adequately causing significant slowing and eventual failure of the system.

The issue was eventually resolved by improving resource allocation and optimizing the application to use other AWS resources when Lambda was saturated.

This event underscores the importance of a few critical aspects - effective monitoring, understanding and predicting user demand trends, ensuring appropriate resource scaling and allocation, and devising a robust disaster recovery plan.

The world of serverless applications can seem overwhelming, but it doesn't have to be. By understanding the different types of disruptions and their root causes, and by implementing appropriate measures to mitigate them, you can ensure smooth functioning of your digital operations on AWS Serverless Application Repository. The keys to managing disruptions are vigilance, preparation, and continual learning. Keep these in your arsenal, and you can weather any digital storm that comes your way.

Chapter 4. Detecting Disruptions: Tools and Techniques

To address disruptions effectively, accurate detection is of paramount importance. There exist numerous tools and techniques within the AWS ecosystem that can help achieve this objective. This chapter discusses these instruments, their functionalities, and how they can be leveraged in detecting disruptions within serverless applications.

4.1. Amazon CloudWatch

Amazon CloudWatch is one of the AWS services that offer seamless detectability for disruptions within serverless applications. It provides actionable insights through collected log and metric data from the resources in danger of being disrupted.

Monitoring your data with CloudWatch can be done in real time, which allows you to react swiftly to changes in your AWS resources. It effectively detects erroneous operational behavior and levels of resource utilization which could cause disruptions.

To successfully implement CloudWatch for disruption detection, you need to set alarms that trigger notifications or automated actions when there's an anomaly detected within your system. These alarms are designed to respond to metrics crossing a specified threshold—an essential part of disruption detection.

4.2. Amazon X-Ray Service

Amazon X-Ray Service offers key insights into user behavior and maps the relationships between the various services used in your application. It provides a visual analysis of your applications, making it clear where and how any request was processed.

By using X-Ray, you can trace requests from end-to-end, even when the requests transit through different AWS services or microservices. Developing a comprehensive X-Ray tracing strategy will help you identify and isolate slow-performing parts of your application, thus allowing for precise disruption detection.

4.3. AWS Step Functions

Step Functions coordinate the different AWS services into serverless workflows, thus delivering seamless application integration. When workflow executions don't go as expected, detecting and rectifying the disruptions is crucial.

The service enables you to track the steps of your execution in near real-time with the help of CloudWatch. Step Functions also offer the ability to manage error handling, retries, and this coordinated reactions can help resume a disrupted workflow, thereby reducing application downtime.

4.4. AWS Lambda and Exception Handling

AWS Lambda is a cornerstone of the Serverless framework of AWS where you can execute your code without provisioning resources. Lambda-based applications often consist of function chains and selecting the right logging and error stack tracing strategy is essential.

Uncaught exceptions and timeouts can disrupt serverless lambda executions. By capturing these, you can detect disruptions early. AWS Lambda automatically monitors functions on your behalf and reports metrics via Amazon CloudWatch.

4.5. Amazon EventBridge

Amazon EventBridge is a serverless event bus service that ingests data from various sources, processes it, and sends it to your AWS destinations. It can listen for specific events, store them, and take automated actions, which serve as an excellent support basis for detecting disruptions.

To set up disruption detection, you can create a custom rule to listen to system or application events, and combine it with Amazon SNS topic to send notifications whenever an event matches the pre-defined criteria, signaling the possible disruptions

4.6. Amazon SNS for Notifications

Whenever disruptions are detected by any of the aforementioned tools, alerting the right teams becomes crucial. Amazon Simple Notification Service (SNS) allows you to handle this part of disruption management.

By integrating CloudWatch and SNS, you can have notifications delivered to your inboxes or phones whenever an event exceeds your threshold. This allows you to act on disruptions promptly, ensuring smooth operations.

Now that you know about the tools and techniques for detecting disruptions, the next step is learning to use these effectively to manage and mitigate such situations.

In the end, remember that disruptions are an integral part of the digital landscape. Thus, having a robust detection mechanism for serverless applications will help you maintain your application performance and, ultimately, your business continuity.

Chapter 5. Strategies for Managing Disruptions

It is essential to tackle disruptions head-on when it comes to the AWS Serverless Application Repository. A well-devised strategy will help in managing these disturbances, ensuring minimum interruption in service, and maintaining an optimal digital experience for all end-users. This chapter will explore such strategies in detail, focusing on both reactive and preventive methods.

5.1. Understanding the Nature of Disruptions

Before diving into specific strategies to manage disruptions, it's imperative to understand the nature and cause of these disruptions. Disruptions in AWS Serverless Applications can stem from a variety of sources, including but not limited to code bugs, system overload, inconsistent dependencies, or even a failure in the underlying AWS services.

AWS services are generally reliable with built-in redundancies and failover mechanisms, but no system is immune to failures. Therefore, it is advisable to plan for disruptions and have well-defined strategies to mitigate their effects. By understanding the potential sources of disruptions, companies can be better equipped to respond and recover from them.

5.2. Proactive Monitoring

To effectively manage disruptions, awareness is key. Proactive monitoring of the system is necessary to observe and detect abnormalities or system breaks. It allows the operations team to record trends, detect anomalies, and track system health. Serverless Framework Pro and AWS CloudWatch are great tools to use for monitoring AWS Serverless Applications. These tools provide insights into system performance and can issue alerts when predefined thresholds are met, allowing quick response to disruptions as they occur.

5.3. Debugging and Testing Applications

Another important strategy for managing disruptions is the regular debugging and testing of applications. This involves unit tests, performance tests, stress tests, and other testing types. By performing routine checks and maintaining updated application versions, you minimize the risk of disruptions.

AWS Lambda provides tools for debugging and AWS Step Functions offer visual workflows to further simplify the debugging process. Be sure to replicate the production environment closely during these checks to anticipate real world scenarios and catch potential points of failure.

5.4. Implementing Redundancy

One key aspect of managing disruptions is building redundancy into your applications. By spreading the risk among multiple instances or resources, the impact of any one disruption can be minimized. For AWS Serverless Applications, implementing multiple AWS Lambda functions, S3 buckets, or DynamoDB tables for backup can be very useful in disruption management.

5.5. Automating Rollbacks

Mistakes are inevitable, and after the deployment of new versions of your serverless application, disruptions can occur due to unforeseen bugs or incompatibilities. To counter this, companies should automate rollbacks to previous stable versions of their application if critical failures are detected in the system. With AWS CodeDeploy, setting up an automated rollback process is straightforward and can help mitigate the downtime associated with serverless application disruptions.

5.6. Enhancing Security

Good security practices are also intrinsic to disruption management. This includes managing access rights, encrypting sensitive data, utilizing secure AWS services, and regularly monitoring AWS security metrics. By enhancing security, many disruptions, such as vulnerabilities exploited or a breach in the cloud architecture, can also be averted.

AWS provides several tools such as AWS Identity and Access Management (IAM), AWS Security Hub, and AWS Shield for helping AWS Serverless Applications stay secure.

5.7. Building a Disaster Recovery Plan

Lastly, every company needs a robust disaster recovery plan that details steps to be taken in the event of major disruptions. The AWS Well-Architected Framework gives good direction on how to build a disaster recovery plan for serverless applications. Automating recovery tasks, regularly backing up data, and conducting disaster recovery drills are practices worth considering.

To conclude, the key to managing disruptions in AWS Serverless Applications lies in proactive measures tempered with swift, informed, reactive solutions when issues arise. Monitoring, testing, adding redundancy, automating rollbacks, enhancing security, and having a disaster recovery plan are crucial components of this process. By mastering these strategies, businesses can ensure smooth operation of their AWS serverless applications and espouse a culture of quick recovery and resilience in the face of digital storms.

Chapter 6. Case Study Analysis: Real World Disruption Management

In the realm of AWS Serverless Application Repository, disruptions are inevitable. Be it due to software bugs, overloaded systems, or even natural disasters, these hurdles cause considerable interruptions in business continuity and smooth customer experience. However, understanding these disruptions, preparing for potential pitfalls, and reacting with appropriate damage control measures are key to navigating these digital storms. To illuminate these ideas further, we bring two real-world case studies of disruption management from renowned organizations: SystemMax Inc. and Albacore Holdings.

6.1. SystemMax Inc. – Preventive Measures against Ransomware Attacks

SystemMax Inc., a global retail company, had an e-commerce application deployed on the AWS Serverless Application Repository. The application saw high volumes of traffic, equivalent to hundreds of thousands of requests per second during peak hours.

In June 2020, SystemMax was hit by what appeared to be a ransomware attack that caused the application to fail, resulting in significant loss of revenue, as well as tarnishing their brand reputation. The management team at SystemMax decided to conduct a thorough post-incident analysis to prevent any future attacks of this nature.

The root cause was identified to be a lack of proper guardrails to control the serverless application environment. To mitigate such situations, SystemMax adopted Amazon API Gateway usage plans and throttling. They set a limit on the rate at which an individual developer could call APIs. The company also used AWS WAF (Web Application Firewall) to protect APIs from common web exploits and AWS Shield for handling massive DDoS attacks.

The results were remarkable. When a similar attempted attack happened a few months later, the application was able to withstand the pressure, resulting in no downtime. This incident illustrates the power of proactive disruption management in the AWS serverless environment.

6.2. Albacore Holdings - Robust Disaster Recovery with AWS

Albacore Holdings operated a major part of their business via an application hosted on the AWS Serverless Application Repository. Their application took in account various financial transactions, and was catalytic in generating revenue for the company.

In November 2021, a severe earthquake in the Pacific Region knocked out many data centers and therefore caused considerable disruptions in the operations of Albacore's application. This led to financial losses and a significant disruption in the client services. In response to this disaster, Albacore identified the need for a robust disaster recovery methodology.

Albacore Holdings decided to utilize the AWS Serverless Application Model (SAM)'s built-in deployment capabilities, along with AWS Step Functions to orchestrate recovery routines and AWS CloudWatch for pinpointing the start of disruptions.

They diverted their workloads to backup data centers using Route53 and AWS Lambda, which allowed them to salvage most of their operations. The company was able to recover and restore service within few hours, immensely reducing lost productivity and client impact.

The resilience of Albacore's application in the face of a natural disaster demonstrated the importance of having a comprehensive disaster recovery strategy when managing disruptions in serverless applications.

These cases illustrate the need for businesses to not only focus on developing serverless applications but also to be agile in managing and mitigating disruptions. By adopting preventive measures, like improving guardrails and implementing robust disaster recovery planning, businesses can strive to maintain their operations even amidst unforeseen incidents.

Each of the businesses in these case studies has made suitable alterations specific to their challenges. It is crucial that when designing your disruption management strategy, you consider the unique aspects of your own serverless application, the potential points of failure, and devise strategies tailored to your specific needs. This is not a one-size-fits-all situation, but a journey that needs to be embarked upon with care and precision. Your understanding and mitigation of potential disruptions can be the difference between emerging stronger or succumbing in the face of digital storms.

Chapter 7. Effective Monitoring of Serverless Applications

Monitoring your serverless applications effectively is your best defense against disruptions. This involves a range of activities, from analyzing logs and metrics to setting up alerts and alarms. In the following section, we'll unpack best practices on how to do this efficiently.

7.1. Understanding the Importance of Monitoring

Thanks to the abstraction level provided by serverless architectures, you don't have to worry about infrastructure-related concerns. However, this doesn't mean you can afford to be lax about monitoring your applications. Some ask, "If the serverless provider manages the infrastructure, why should I bother monitoring?"

To answer this question, let's clarify the distinction between infrastructure and application monitoring. While serverless providers monitor the infrastructure to maximize uptime and performance, the developer maintains the onus responsibility to track the application to ensure it is running as expected.

7.2. Monitoring in the Serverless Context

In traditional monolithic architectures, the focus was mostly put on monitoring hardware such as CPU utilization, disk usage, and memory allocations. But with serverless architectures, these aspects are offloaded to the service provider.

For serverless applications, monitoring should be focused on:

- Function execution times
- Error rates
- Retries
- Cold start durations
- Timeout occurrences

7.3. Choosing the Right Monitoring Tools

AWS provides several tools that you can leverage in your monitoring endeavors, such as AWS CloudWatch, AWS X-Ray, and AWS CloudTrail.

AWS CloudWatch: Allows developers to collect and track metrics, collect and monitor log files, set alarms, and automatically react to changes in AWS resources.

AWS X-Ray: Provides insights into your application's behavior by tracing requests from start to end and shows a map of your application's underlying components.

AWS CloudTrail: Enables governance, compliance, and operational and risk auditing of your AWS account by tracking AWS account activity.

For more complex needs, third-party monitoring tools such as Datadog, Serverless Framework Dashboard, and Thundra might be more suitable.

7.4. Setting up Monitoring in AWS CloudWatch

Firstly, you need to set up monitoring by creating log groups in CloudWatch for each of your Serverless applications.

Step 1	Navigate to AWS CloudWatch Logs in your AWS Console.
Step 2	Choose "Create log group" and enter a name for your log group.
Step 3	Assign the necessary roles and permissions.
Step 4	Attach the necessary subscription filters.

After your log groups are set up, you can navigate to the relevant logs when error notifications come in.

7.5. Defining Alarms and Anomalies in AWS CloudWatch

Alarms and anomalies are essential to any robust monitoring endeavor. AWS CloudWatch enables you to set both.

To set up an alarm, you navigate to the metrics section of CloudWatch, choose the desired metrics, set the conditions for when an alarm should be triggered, and set the action that should occur when the alarm goes off.

Anomaly detection, contrastingly, uses machine learning to detect aberrant behavior. To set up anomaly detection, you need to navigate to the metric where you'd like anomaly detection and choose "Anomaly detection."

As you have an understanding of what aspects to monitor, and the tools to use, set sail as the captain of your serverless monitoring adventure. Remember that effective monitoring is a continuous process. It needs regular refinement and adjustment to meet evolving business needs and cases. The name of the game is staying vigilant and proactive – this is how you keep disruptions in check and deliver a seamless digital experience.

Chapter 8. Troubleshooting AWS Serverless Applications: A Step-By-Step Guide

In our stroll through the paths of managing AWS Serverless Applications, we dive into a nuts-and-bolts perspective—troubleshooting. No journey is seamless, and hitches are inevitable. The aim is to transition from reacting to those glitches to a proactive mitigation strategy.

Understanding AWS Serverless Applications ===

The AWS Serverless Application Repository (SAR) is a managed service that makes it easy for developers to create, share, and deploy serverless applications. However, when issues arise, it is important to know where to begin troubleshooting.

These applications are composed of components like AWS Lambda functions, Amazon API Gateway APIs, DynamoDB tables, and more, each of which can run into its own unique challenges. Troubleshooting a serverless application means comprehending these parts well and evaluating where the problem might stem from.

Identifying Issues through Logs ===

Serverless applications often do not run in a traditional server where you can just check the logs. However, AWS provides its own service, AWS CloudWatch, to tackle this very issue. Logs are the first point of contact when an issue arises.

Here's how to access them:

1. Go to the AWS Management Console.
2. Open the CloudWatch console.

3. In the navigation pane, click on Logs.

4. Click on the name of the log group that you want to view.

It is essential to filter and search through multiple log streams to track down the source of an issue.

Understanding AWS X-Ray for Debugging ===

AWS X-Ray is another service by AWS that helps in gaining insights into your applications. It provides an end-to-end view of requests as they travel through your application and shows a map of your application's underlying components. By using X-Ray, you can analyze latencies in your applications and trace the individual requests.

Setting up X-Ray with Lambda needs some permissions that you only set in your IAM roles.

Here's the process:

1. Provide the AWSXRayDaemonWriteAccess managed policy to your function's execution role.

2. Instrument your code by requiring the AWS X-Ray SDK and patching modules (like the AWS SDK) that you want to trace.

3. Open the Trace view in the X-Ray console to view traces of requests.

Managing Failed Executions ===

AWS Lambda automatically retries the function for some types of errors, such as throttles and timeouts. However, if the function throws an unhandled error or is not triggered correctly, you need to manually troubleshoot the problem.

Here's how to identify why it failed:

1. Use the AWS CLI or SDKs to catch the error message from failed invocations.

2. Identify whether there was an issue with your code or AWS services by seeing if other functions or apps had a similar failure.

3. Use CloudWatch Logs to monitor the operations.

Debugging Performance Issues ===

AWS Lambda keeps the function loaded for a period of time, which we can exploit for performance troubleshooting. Performance can be hindered by cold-starts or memory size.

Here's how you can troubleshoot performance issues:

1. Monitor metrics in CloudWatch to understand performance over time.

2. Use AWS CLI or SDKs to see how long the function took to run.

3. Increase the function's memory size and test to check for improved execution time.

Handling Errors in the API Gateway ===

If your service has an API Gateway and it fails to call your Lambda function, the issue might rest with the setup of the API Gateway. Each step in the API Gateway-to-Lambda flow can have errors and must be checked separately.

Here's how you can handle this:

1. Define mapping templates for your API's integration request and integration response.

2. Define the mapping template for the method response.

3. Check for syntax errors in the mapping template.

4. Isolate the issue by mapping out the entire API Gateway-to-

Lambda flow.

Coping with Application Errors in DynamoDB ===

DynamoDB is a key component of many serverless applications built on AWS. Applications are dependent on the successful execution of their DynamoDB database operations.

Here's how you can deal with these errors:

1. Use CloudWatch metrics to diagnose DynamoDB performance.

2. Handle individual error codes by building robust retry policies using exponential backoffs.

3. Use the AWS Command Line Interface (CLI) or libraries in AWS SDKs to test your code against specific error conditions while in development.

4. Apply DynamoDB best practices to avoid common errors.

In conclusion, troubleshooting serverless applications consists of managing all individual components and being vigilant in monitoring logs and metrics. Always ensure you've got access to vast resources available through AWS documentation and forums to keep your applications running without trouble.

Chapter 9. Disruption Prevention: Proactive Practices for Smooth Operations

Adopting a proactive stance towards disruption management is paramount in ensuring smooth operations. This section will explore the key elements and practices that will help maintain your AWS Serverless Application Repository up and running with minimal disruptions.

9.1. Prerequisites: Familiarizing Yourself with the AWS Serverless Landscape

To successfully manage and prevent disruptions of your serverless applications, you should first be conversant with the architecture and components of the AWS Serverless Landscape. At the core, we have Amazon's AWS Lambda service, a compute service that lets you execute your code without provisioning or managing servers. Accompanying AWS Lambda is the use of various event sources that automatically trigger the functions. Familiar event sources include AWS S3 for storage, AWS DynamoDB for databases, and many more.

9.2. Establish Robust Monitoring and Logging Practices

Robust monitoring is a critical element of disruption prevention. It is crucial to collect and analyze logs and metrics, so you are aware of what is happening in your environment. With AWS, you can utilize services like Amazon CloudWatch and AWS X-Ray.

Amazon CloudWatch is an observability service that collects monitoring and operational data in the form of logs, metrics, and events, providing a unified view of AWS resources, applications, and services. AWS X-Ray, on the other hand, provides insights into the behavior of your applications, enabling you to analyze and debug your serverless applications more efficiently.

Here are some proactive practices to consider:

- Set up alarms for unusual activity: CloudWatch lets you set up alarms to notify you of any suspicious or unusual activity. As soon as anomalous behavior is identified, you receive an alert, enabling you to address the issue promptly.

- Create custom dashboards: With CloudWatch Dashboards, you can create customizable home pages to monitor resources across regions and accounts.

- Trace request paths: AWS X-Ray enables you to visualize and trace requests from beginning to end. This can help identify bottlenecks or issues that could potentially disrupt the smooth functioning of your application.

FTP1::[Footnote: You can explore more about AWS Monitoring and Logging best practices at the official AWS documentation.]

9.3. Optimize Error Handling and Retry Policies

One essential part of managing disruptions in serverless applications is learning how to handle errors effectively. AWS provides various error handling and retry policies that you can take advantage of to add resilience to your applications. For instance, AWS Lambda will automatically retry failed function invocations, while Amazon SQS and other event source mappings allow customizing the retry policy.

You can also use Dead-Letter Queues (DLQs) to save events that could not be processed for further analysis. Additionally, consider setting up an alarm on DLQ to get notified when an event lands there, indicating a failure in your primary function.

Some areas to focus on include:

- Configuring appropriate timeout settings: If your serverless function is running longer than necessary, it may be an indication of a problem. Configure your function's timeout setting based on its expected execution time.

- Consider exponential backoff and jitter for retries: This strategy increases the wait time between retries exponentially to minimize the risk of further failures.

FTP2::[Footnote: You can refer to the official AWS guide on AWS Lambda Retry Behavior.]

9.4. Resiliency Through Architectural Best Practices

Good architecture is foundational to a resilient system. The Well-Architected Framework, defined by AWS, presents a set of architectural best practices for designing and operating reliable, secure, efficient, and cost-effective systems in the cloud. By using this framework, you can mitigate the effects of service or infrastructure disruptions and prevent them from occurring in the first place.

Some noteworthy principles from this framework include:

- Implementing a multi-tier architecture: This involves separating different parts of your application into distinct tiers or layers.

This way, if one tier is compromised, it doesn't immediately affect the others.

- Applying the principle of least privilege: This principle recommends that every module (such as a process, a user, or a program) should have the least amount of privilege necessary to perform its function.

- Designing for failover: A failover architecture enables your system to switch over to a redundant or standby system in the event of a failure with minimal impact on service.

FTP3::[Footnote: The AWS Well-Architected Framework provides a comprehensive set of best practices and principles for designing and operating your system: https://aws.amazon.com/architecture/well-architected/]

Disruption prevention in the AWS Serverless Application Repository is an ongoing journey, and the guidelines outlined in this chapter provide a good starting point. By understanding your environment, monitoring it effectively, handling errors appropriately, and architecting your serverless applications for resilience, you can greatly minimize disruptions and ensure smooth operations.

Chapter 10. Emergency Response: Navigating Serverless Application Crises

Such is the nature of the digital landscape; unforeseen circumstances and crises can disrupt the smooth operation of even the most robust and well-designed serverless applications. Before panic can infiltrate your team, it's crucial to have a clear, effective emergency response procedure in place to navigate these application crises. This chapter provides careful guidelines to help you be well-prepared for managing disruptions in serverless AWS applications, drawing on real-world examples and expert insight.

10.1. Gathering a Competent Response Team

The first fundamental step to take on the road towards mastering emergency management is assembling a competent response team. This team should be made up of engineers, IT personnel, and individuals proficient enough with AWS serverless architecture to quickly respond and mitigate risks when they arise. A communication liaison should also be assigned, whose role will be to communicate updates to necessary stakeholders.

Alongside technical proficiency and communication skills, team members should be quick-thinking and agile to ensure problems can be swiftly resolved. A strong project manager should be appointed to oversee the team, ensuring smooth coordination. The project manager ensures that problems are efficiently addressed and takes necessary escalation steps if they cannot be resolved at the team's level.

10.2. Establishing a Proactive Monitoring System

Another key strategy for effectively handling disturbances in the AWS Serverless Application Repository is setting up proactive monitoring measures. Based on Amazon's CloudWatch service, this offers real-time monitoring for AWS resources used by your applications.

With this tool, our response team can set alarms, track errors, analyze logs, gather metrics, and create custom dashboards for a bird's-eye view of your application. It empowers teams with real-time data on how applications and services are performing, so that potential issues can be addressed before they turn into larger disruptions affecting end-users.

10.3. Crises Communication Plan

Effective communication is as crucial as technical proficiency during an emergency. It's paramount to establish a transparent, concise crisis communication plan that ensures all teams are in sync, leadership and decision-makers are informed, and users are updated with relevant information.

A best practice here involves designating a communication lead, who will bridge technical and non-technical teams, act as the liaison to leadership, and help plan and execute user-facing announcements. Their role is to strip tech-heavy complexities to relatable language that can be understood by all parties.

10.4. Incident Triage and Analysis

During an emergency, incidents need to be systematically assessed and prioritized—this process is known as triage. A significant triage component involves immediate threat assessment, gauging the immediate impact on the end-users, and paying attention to the incident's potential growth.

The team should then look at the logs in CloudWatch and application error messages to understand what might have triggered the issue. Using tools like AWS X-Ray to trace requests can also provide insight into the problem's source.

To facilitate faster incident analysis:

- Standardize your logging format across all services
- Include customer ID in your logs (where applicable)
- Include a unique request ID in logs for correlation

10.5. Recovering from Disaster

After identifying and understanding the threat accurately, the team should focus on returning your system to its functional state. During this phase, teams could roll back the application to its last functional state using AWS CodeDeploy, or push a hotfix for a code-related issue.

In a more comprehensive disaster scenario (e.g. a significant database crash), you might have to recover from an AWS backup. It's crucial to regularly back up your resources in Amazon S3 and use automated snapshot tools for databases.

Remember, the goal during this phase is to minimize downtime and prevent data loss. As thus, testing your recovery strategies and conducting regular drills on recovery operations ensures your team is prepared to execute in an actual disaster scenario.

10.6. Post Mortem Analysis

Once the issue has been resolved, the team should conduct a post-mortem analysis to glean insights about the crisis, document exactly what happened, and find out how to prevent similar issues in the future. This should ideally be an obligation, not an option.

Critical elements to cover include:

- What caused the emergency?

- How it was diagnosed?

- Measures taken to fix it

- How long it took to respond, recover, and resolve

- How to prevent similar situations in the future

Implementing and documenting these lessons from every post-mortem fortifies and improves your crisis management over time.

10.7. Final Words on Managing Crisis

Preparing for disruption and effectively handling crises is a dynamic, not a definitive, process. As you continue to improve your AWS serverless applications, your emergency response procedures should also evolve. Conducting regular drills, ongoing training of your response team, documenting and learning from every incident, and being vigilant about the health of your application—these all contribute to the resilience and reliability of your digital operation.

Remember, the ultimate goal of an emergency response process isn't just about facing crises—it's to ensure a seamless and uninterrupted customer experience, even when a digital storm hits.

Chapter 11. Future Outlook: Next-Generation Practices in AWS Serverless Applications

Embracing the future entails understanding the forthcoming trends and technologies poised to redefine aspects pertaining to AWS Serverless Applications. These generational shifts promise enhanced operational efficiencies, reduction of costs, and unparalleled scalability, marking a pivotal aspect of modern business strategies.

11.1. Next-Generation AWS Serverless Architecture

There is an imminent shift occurring in the architectural principles of AWS serverless applications. Traditional serverless architectures focused primarily on monolithic designs, neglecting some of the cost and scalability benefits of microservices architecture. However, a new generation of AWS serverless applications is emerging that embraces the microservices design pattern. Monoliths will give way to microservices, where the application is decoupled into smaller, independently deployable services, each running its unique process and communicating via HTTP APIs or messaging queues.

The move towards microservices is driven by an increasing need for businesses to scale their applications quickly. Scalability, usually a strength of serverless architectures, can be curtailed if the application is composed of a single, unwieldy monolith. Microservices, on the other hand, offer improved scalability options by allowing each service to scale independently in response to demand, resulting in more cost-effective scaling solutions.

Another aspect of next-generation AWS serverless architecture is observability. It is the ability to understand the state of systems by observing outputs or the result of system execution. As serverless applications move to distributed architectures, monitoring, logging, and debugging grow increasingly complex. Future AWS services will aim to embed observability at a deeper level, giving developers immediate insight into application behavior without needing to physically interact with servers, containers, or other resources.

11.2. Leveraging Automation for Improved Efficiency

Automation is at the heart of serverless computing, and its significance will only grow. More businesses will move towards an Infrastructure as Code (IaC) model, where infrastructure is provisioned and managed using machine-readable definition files, rather than by clicking around in the management console.

Advanced AWS services and toolkits, such as the AWS Cloud Development Kit (CDK) or AWS Serverless Application Model (SAM), will gain further prevalence. These toolkits allow developers to define serverless applications easily in code - which can then be automatically deployed, managed, and even versioned. This shift will lead to significantly improved deployment times, reduced error rates, and effortless scaling.

Additionally, automation will play an increasing role in maintaining serverless application security. Automated security controls, such as AWS IAM Access Analyzer, will become a staple in serverless stack configurations. Security checks will be integrated into deployment pipelines, allowing for detection and rectification of vulnerabilities in the application code or the serverless infrastructure, further bolstering cloud security.

11.3. The Evolution of Event-Driven Computing

Event-driven computing is the heart of serverless: code executions are triggered by events such as changes to data in a database, requests to an API, or files uploaded to a storage bucket. However, the paradigm is evolving: the future of AWS serverless includes more refined event-driven computing models.

To cater to complex, multistep workflows, AWS Step Functions will be utilized more extensively. This service lets you orchestrate several AWS Lambda functions into serverless workflows, simplifying the coordination of components in serverless applications.

Developers will also have more control over event triggering. At present, Lambda invocations are often based on high-level AWS service events. Future developments may give developers the power to define their own resource events. This granularity of event definition allows developers to better handle various types of events, driving more responsive and reliable applications.

11.4. Continued Cost Optimization

Cost efficiency is another area of future progress. While serverless architectures are cheap to run, unexpected costs can occur due to inefficiencies or errors in the architecture. As the serverless landscape matures, new and improved methods for cost optimization will surface.

One method is to fine-tune the balance between cost and performance, by choosing the perfect configuration for each Lambda function. Future toolkits will allow for precise control over aspects such as memory allocation and timeout settings, allowing developers to strike the right balance for their specific use case.

Another potential optimization is to conserve costs in development or test environments, such as tearing down serverless infrastructure when not in use.

11.5. New Programming Paradigms and Runtime Improvements

Next-generation AWS serverless applications will support diverse programming language runtimes, potentially including new languages or sandboxed execution environments. More attention will be given to managing ephemeral state across invocations. As a result, functions themselves might become more predictable and faster due to improvements in cold start latency. These developments will enable developers to structure their code in ways best suited to their specific needs and architectural requirements.

As AWS serverless technologies become increasingly sophisticated, advance in their lifecycle, and expand their application scope, it's imperative that businesses adapt and align their strategies with these innovative trends. A fundamental understanding of these forthcoming patterns will allow enterprises to create proactive and well-informed action plans, ensuring they remain at the forefront of the digital revolution.